Things That Keep Us Warm

WRITTEN BY
Louise Flaherty

Published by Inhabit Education | www.inhabiteducation.com

Inhabit Education (Iqaluit), P.O. Box 2129, Iqaluit, Nunavut, X0A 1H0
(Toronto), 191 Eglinton Avenue East, Suite 302, Toronto, Ontario, M4P 1K1

Printed in Canada.

ISBN: 978-1-77266-055-5

This is a hat.

These are parkas.

These are kamiks.

These are socks.

This is a qulliq.

This is a Coleman stove.

This is a house.